Table of Contents

PREFACE

Let me ask you an inquiry are you satisfied with your health? Do you ever think suppose I obtain heart cancer, stroke or assault? Do you have loved one that has diabetes or Alzheimer's?

At the beginning of any one of these problems was high blood sugar level. There are many scientific papers that define this in wonderful information. I list a few of the papers at the references area of this publication.

Sugar is surprisingly tasty, cheap and addicting. This is why it discovers its place on ingredient checklist of several foods you really do not expect to see sugar ever. Having sugar in the food practically guarantees it will certainly be yummy and that you will crave it extra.

Chocolate is giant of anti-oxidants as well as nutrients, but only if it is done effectively with real cacao and also without sugar.

This publication is terrific for you if you are cutting the quantity of sugar in your diet as well as wish to have all the healthy antioxidants from chocolate.

You may merely wish to consume less calories while taking pleasure in the wonderful life. (You can be conserving at least 773 calories per typical delicious chocolate bar).

Did you recognize that cholesterol in blood ends up being unsafe once it reacts with sugar in the blood? That was enough for me to stop making use of sugar in my food preparation.

Did you recognize that fungal infections and also cancer cells feed upon sugar? Put simply consume pleasant simply don't make use of sugar.

It is possible, Nature provided us with amazing all-natural pleasant resources that are not hazardous to our bodies.

This book will certainly reveal you just how to make healthy and balanced antioxidant abundant Delicious chocolate customized to Your taste.

Directions in this book are:
Detailed guidelines-- extremely simple to adhere to
You can customize your delicious chocolate to suit your preference
No tempering ever-- I will show you my secret way for excellent snap chocolate without toughening up (unless you take pleasure in doing toughening up).

WHY IS SUGAR BAD FOR YOU?

Sugar was limited through history. To make points worse the more stressed you are much more sugar you will certainly crave.

Too much sugar interferes with your intestine pancreatic, health and wellness as well as liver health and wellness. Sugar in your blood can enhance chance of blocked arteries and also probability of heart attack.

In easy terms sugar is actually poor for you. Great news is - you can still consume all the desserts you are utilized to, just without sugar. This publication is all about making 100% natural Delicious Antioxidant Rich Sugar Free Chocolate without any Tempering. (Should have uppercase).

CHOCOLATE ORIGIN:

Maya individuals of Central America were the initial individuals to make delicious chocolate over a thousand years ago.

Maya believed delicious chocolate was gift of Gods and also enjoyed it daily. Please note Maya did not have any kind of sugar to sweeten the delicious chocolate and also they were utilizing just water to make it. It is believed that they likewise added chilies to the cacao drink.

Chocolate arrived to Europe through Spanish conquerors. Throughout 17th century delicious chocolate was taking over Italy, Germany as well as France.

Englishmen began taking in delicious chocolate. English people have actually included milk, eggs, as well as alcohol to the initial delicious chocolate drink.

Chocolate got here to The United States and Canada in 1700s. President Thomas Jefferson was a big fan of delicious chocolate.

When it was discovered exactly how to draw out chocolate butter out of chocolate paste and just how to deal with chocolate with alkaline salts (Dutching), Modern age for chocolate began in Holland. This was wonderful for Delicious chocolate market but however it got rid of most of the health and wellness beneficial antioxidants.

Chocolate ended up being easier to mix with milk and also sugar and it was simpler to put right into mold and mildews. Taste buds were delighted however it is not that terrific for the remainder of our body.

HEALTH BENEFITS

Cacao has two times as many antioxidants as merlot and almost three times as lots of antioxidants as green tea. (compared per weight).

Cacao anti-oxidants are flavonoids. Flavonoids (from cacao) have anti-viral; anti-cancer; anti-allergic and also anti-inflammatory impact. This is the reason why evaluation of medical tests published in "Nutrition as well as metabolism" revealed that cacao may help shield versus cardiac arrest as well as stroke.

A lot of powerful flavonoid (sort of antioxidant) is Epicatechin. Epicatechin has actually been revealed to boost nitric oxide manufacturing which assists boost blood flow and also aids flexibility of capillary. Epicatechin improves insulin level of sensitivity which assists to reduce blood sugar levels as well as is really helpful if you are struggling with diabetic issues. Epicatechin likewise lowers cholesterol levels as well as generally improves mind and also heart wellness. Do you require much more reasons to make your very own delicious chocolate from square one from cacao?

Well allow's explore few a lot more health advantages; antioxidants from cacao lower cost-free extreme damage in the body which may decrease danger of developing cancer cells. Please note cacao has even more anti-oxidants than acai, goji berries and blueberries.

Cacao can improve your mood by increasing natural chemicals in your brain. No wonder delicious chocolate is standard Valentine's day gift.

Cacao is excellent source of iron, zinc, manganese, and potassium simply to name a few minerals.

CACAO OR COCOA?

Yes, there is a difference.

Cacao is product that is stemmed from cacao beans-- from the cacao tree. You can have cacao nibs, cacao butter, cacao mass as well as powder.

Raw cacao powder is cold pressed from unroasted cacao beans. This way Cacao powder maintains living enzymes as well as anti-oxidants that are most health useful.

Chocolate powder on the other hand has actually been baked. This results in milder preference yet reduces enzymes and anti-oxidants and consequently health and wellness benefits.

You can still enjoy it as long as you are aware that it will be mostly to please your taste buds and except improving your wellness. Since your chocolate will certainly not have any kind of sugar it will not be damaging to your health.

HOW TO SWEETEN YOUR CHOCOLATE

Enjoy sugar free delicious chocolate on your terms and just how you like it. The best and most convenient sugar to work with in my point of view are:.

One mug of sugar has 773 calories, Stevia has 0 calories. My recipes use just the pure 100 % Stevia removes that offers you impressive results. Make certain your Stevia is 100 % Stevia plant essence as there are many products on the market that use different fillers which may offer bitter preference to your chocolate.

2.100% birch extracted xylitol. Exactly how is that- you can eat wonderful and not fret concerning your teeth ...

Please note: there are xylitol extracts from different sources, try to get one extracted removed birch.

INGREDIENTS

BASIC INGREDIENTS

Cacao powder -.

Or replace with refined cacao Cacao butter-- buttons, wafers or in bloc.

Milk powder or Coconut milk powder if dairy cost-free Stevia, 100 % pure plant removes (no fillers) Natural birch essence xylitol.

Freeze dried out cacao butter - vital ingredient to prevent tempering.

ADVANCED INGREDIENTS

Nuts of your choice Freeze dried fruits Edible shades.

Focused flavor removes Blew Rice-- bitter.

Dry fruit: please be extremely cautious as some fruits have sugarcoated plus dry fruit has plenty of focused sugar that may raise your blood sugar levels.

EQUIPMENT

Kitchen range.
Flavor grinder - you will require to additional grind your milk powder and
xylitol Metal bowl as glass keeps temperature level a lot longer.
Spatula as well as whisk Measuring spoons Chocolate mold and mildews.

Optional:

Sweet fusion or.
Crock-pot if making huge amounts (very helpful if making Healthy chocolate
Holiday presents).

HOW TO MAKE CHOCOLATE:

Make sure you have all of your ingredients ready as process is really quick.

DARK
CHOCOLATE:

Ingredients:

4 oz cacao butter (please measure as cacao butter can be found in many different kinds).

8 table spoons cacao powder (or unsweetened cacao powder of your selection).

1/2 teaspoon 100% pure Stevia essence.

2 table spoons 100% birch extract xylitol - make certain it is finest feasible powder comparable uniformity as icing sugar. If you do not chocolate will certainly be fairly rough.

2 table spoons freeze dried out cacao butter.

Devices:.

Double central heating boiler-- you may utilize pot full of 1-2 fingers of water. Area metal dish with cacao butter in addition to it making sure bottom does not touch the water.

You may melt cacao butter in microwave however see to it you are just utilizing 10 seconds periods and also most affordable possible setting.

Flavor mill: please grind your cacao powder and xylitol to extremely fine.

Metal dish for blending the chocolate metal launches warm quicker contrasted to glass and is much better when making chocolate.

Gauging spoons.

Spatula and blend for mixing chocolate.

If you need chocolate liquid for longer if making use of fragile mold and mildews-- optional, candy maker.

Delicious chocolate mold and mildews-- plastic or silicon; you can also make use of containers that you already contend residence (for example lids from storage space containers).

Instructions.
1. Procedure 4 oz of cacao butter on the scale. You will certainly need to gauge it as you might be using different forms of cacao butter.
2. Grind cacao powder as well as xylitol to super fine making use of seasoning grinder (you might be able to buy superfine cacao powder that will certainly not need any grinding, I still like to grind my xylitol even when it looks penalty).
3. Location cacao butter in dual boiler till thawed. You might select to.

thaw it in microwave. In that situation usage microwave safe bowl and also heat cacao butter in 10 sec periods making certain to stir well in between home heating.

4. When cacao butter is completely melted include 8 table spoons of cacao powder and also blend well with whisk. Make certain all powder is mixed in.
5. Include 1/2 tsp of 100 % pure Stevia remove in powder remove, mix well.
6. Add 2 tbsps of ground Natural Birch remove Xylitol mix once more.
7. Include 2 table spoons of freeze dried cacao butter and mix well.
8. Area back on double boiler and mix till completely integrated (1-2 min).
9. Pour into molds as well as location into refrigerator till established-- 2-3 hours, or over night.
10. ENJOY!

MILK CHOCOLATE:

Ingredients:

4 oz cacao butter.

8 table spoons cacao powder (or unsweetened chocolate powder of your option).

6 table spoons completely dry milk powder - ensure it is finest possible powder similar uniformity as topping sugar. Grind in flavor grinder till it is superfine uniformity. If you don't chocolate might be fairly rough.

1/2 teaspoon 100% pure Stevia essence.

2 table spoons 100% birch remove xylitol - make certain it is finest possible powder similar consistency as icing sugar. If you do not delicious chocolate will certainly be quite grainy.

2 table spoons ice up dried cacao butter.

Devices:.

Dual central heating boiler-- you might make use of pot filled with 1-2 fingers of water. Area steel bowl with cacao butter in addition to it ensuring base does not touch the water.

You may melt cacao butter in microwave but make sure you are only utilizing 10 seconds intervals as well as least expensive possible setup.

Flavor grinder: please grind your cacao powder, milk powder as well as xylitol to super fine.

Metal dish for blending the delicious chocolate. Determining spoons. Spatula and whisk for mixing chocolate.

Candy maker if you require chocolate liquid for longer if making use of fragile mold and mildews-- optional.

Chocolate molds-- plastic or silicon you can use vessels that you already have at house (for example lids from storage space containers).

Directions.
1. Measure 4 oz of cacao butter on the scale. You will certainly have to determine it as you may be utilizing various forms of cacao butter.
2. Grind in spice grinder cacao powder, dry milk powder and xylitol to extremely penalty (you may have the ability to purchase superfine cacao powder that will certainly not require any type of grinding, I still like to grind my xylitol even when it looks penalty).
Location cacao butter in double boiler till thawed. In that situation usage microwave safe bowl as well as warm.

cacao butter in 10 sec intervals making certain to mix well in between home heating.
4. When cacao butter is totally thawed add 8 table spoons of cacao powder and also mix well with whisk. Make sure all powder is blended in.
5. Include 6 table spoons of grinded dry milk powder, mix well.
6. Include 1/2 teaspoon of 100 % pure Stevia remove in powder essence, mix well.
7. Add 2 tbsps of ground All-natural Birch remove Xylitol mix once

more.
8. Include 2 table spoons of freeze dried cacao butter as well as mix well.
9. Place back on double central heating boiler as well as mix till totally integrated (1-2 min).
10. Put right into mold and mildews and location into fridge till established-- 2-3 hrs, or overnight.
11. ENJOY!

VEGAN "MILK" CHOCOLATE:

Ingredients:

4 oz cacao butter.

8 table spoons cacao powder (or bitter cacao powder of your choice).

6 table spoons dry Coconut milk powder - ensure it is finest feasible powder comparable uniformity as icing sugar. Grind in spice mill till it is superfine consistency. If you do not chocolate might be quite rough.

1/2 teaspoon 100% pure Stevia essence.

2 table spoons 100% birch remove xylitol - make certain it is finest possible powder similar consistency as icing sugar. If you do not chocolate will certainly be quite grainy.

2 table spoons freeze dried cacao butter.

Equipment:.

Dual central heating boiler-- you may utilize pot filled with 1-2 fingers of water. Place metal bowl with cacao butter on top of it ensuring bottom does not touch the water.

You may melt cacao butter in microwave however see to it you are just making use of 10 seconds intervals as well as most affordable feasible setting.

Spice grinder: please grind your cacao powder, completely dry Coconut milk powder and xylitol to very penalty (you may have the ability to acquire superfine cacao powder that will not require any type of grinding; I still like to grind my xylitol even when it looks fine).

Metal bowl for blending the chocolate. Determining spoons.
Blend and also spatula for mixing chocolate.

Candy maker if you require chocolate fluid for longer if using fragile mold and mildews-- optional.

Delicious chocolate molds-- plastic or silicon you can utilize vessels that you already have at home (for instance lids from storage containers).

Directions.
1. Action 4 oz of cacao butter on the scale. You will have to measure it as you may be making use of various shapes of cacao butter.
2. Grind in seasoning grinder cacao powder, completely dry coconut milk powder and also xylitol to extremely penalty.
Location cacao butter in dual central heating boiler till thawed. (In that situation usage microwave secure bowl and also.

warm cacao butter in 10 sec intervals seeing to it to stir well between heating.).
4. When cacao butter is entirely melted include 8 table spoons of cacao powder and blend well with whisk. Ensure all powder is mixed in.
5. Add 6 table spoons of dry coconut milk powder, mix well.
6. Add 1/2 tsp of 100 % pure Stevia essence in powder remove, mix well.
7. Add 2 tablespoons of ground All-natural Birch remove Xylitol mix once more.

8. Add 2 table spoons of freeze dried out cacao butter and also blend well.
9. Area back on dual boiler and mix till totally integrated (1-2 min).
10. Pour into mold and mildews and also area right into fridge till set-- 2-3 hours, or over night.
11. ENJOY!

WHITE CHOCOLATE:

Ingredients:

4 oz cacao butter

- 8 table spoons dry milk powder - make sure it is finest possible powder similar consistency as icing sugar. Grind in spice grinder till it is superfine consistency. If you don't chocolate may be quite grainy
- ½ teaspoon 100% pure Stevia extract
- 2 table spoons 100% birch extract xylitol - make sure it is finest possible powder similar consistency as icing sugar. If you can only get in granules grind in spice grinder till it is superfine consistency. If you don't chocolate will be quite grainy. You may choose not to use xylitol if you are sensitive to it.
- 2 table spoons freeze dried cacao butter

Equipment:

Double boiler – you may use pot filled with 1-2 fingers of water. Place metal bowl with cacao butter on top of it making sure bottom does not touch the water.

You may melt cacao butter in microwave but make sure you are only using 10 seconds intervals and lowest possible setting.

Spice grinder: please grind your cacao powder, dry milk powder and xylitol to super fine.

Metal bowl for mixing the chocolate.

Measuring spoons.

Whisk and spatula for mixing chocolate.

Candy maker for keeping chocolate liquid for longer – optional.

Chocolate molds – plastic or silicon you can use vessels that you already have at home (for example lids from storage containers).

Directions
1. Measure 4 oz of cacao butter on the scale. You will have to measure it as you may be using different shapes of cacao butter.
2. Grind in spice grinder dry milk powder and xylitol to super fine.
3. Place cacao butter in double boiler till melted. You may choose to melt it in microwave. In that case use microwave safe bowl and heat cacao butter in 10 sec intervals making sure to stir well between heating.
4. When cacao butter is completely melted add 8 table spoons of dry milk powder and mix well with whisk. Make sure all powder is mixed in.
5. Add ½ teaspoon of 100 % pure Stevia extract in powder extract,

mix well

6. Add 2 tablespoons of ground Natural Birch extract Xylitol mix again
7. Add 2 table spoons of freeze dried cacao butter and mix well
8. Place back on double boiler and mix till fully combined (1-2 min)
9. Pour into molds and place into fridge till set – 2-3 hours, or overnight
10. ENJOY!

VEGAN WHITE CHOCOLATE:

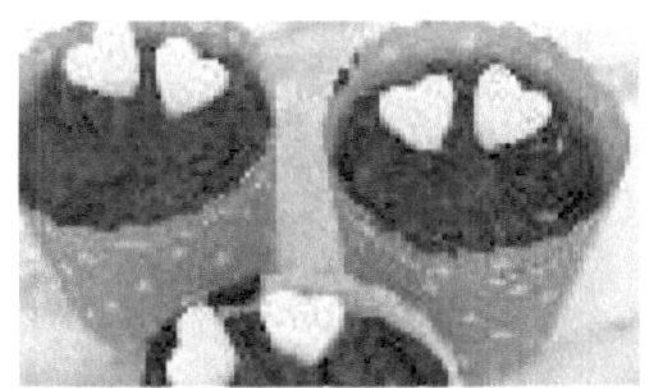

Ingredients:

- 4 oz cacao butter
- 8 table spoons dry Coconut milk powder - make sure it is finest possible powder similar consistency as icing sugar. Grind in spice grinder till it is superfine consistency. If you don't chocolate may be quite grainy
- ½ teaspoon 100% pure Stevia extract
- 2 table spoons 100% birch extract xylitol - make sure it is finest possible powder similar consistency as icing sugar. If you can only get in granules grind in spice grinder till it is superfine consistency. If you don't chocolate will be quite grainy. You may choose not to use xylitol if you are sensitive to it.
- 2 table spoons freeze dried cacao butter

Equipment:

Double boiler – you may use pot filled with 1-2 fingers of water. Place metal bowl with cacao butter on top of it making sure bottom does not touch the water.

You may melt cacao butter in microwave but make sure you are only using 10 seconds intervals and lowest possible setting.

Spice grinder: please grind your dry coconut milk powder and xylitol to super fine.

Metal bowl for mixing the chocolate.

Measuring spoons.

Whisk and spatula for mixing chocolate.

Candy maker for making chocolate liquid for longer – optional.

Chocolate molds – plastic or silicon you can use vessels that you already have at home (for example lids from storage containers).

Directions
1. Measure 4 oz of cacao butter on the scale. You will have to measure it as you may be using different shapes of cacao butter.
2. Grind in spice grinder dry coconut milk powder and xylitol to super fine.
3. Place cacao butter in double boiler till melted. You may choose to melt it in microwave. In that case use microwave safe bowl and heat cacao butter in 10 sec intervals making sure to stir well between heating.
4. When cacao butter is completely melted add 8 table spoons of dry coconut milk powder and mix well with whisk. Make sure all powder is mixed in.
5. Add ½ teaspoon of 100 % pure Stevia extract in powder extract, mix well
6. Add 2 tablespoons of ground Natural Birch extract Xylitol mix again
7. Add 2 table spoons of freeze dried cacao butter and mix well
8. Place back on double boiler and mix till fully combined (1-2 min)

9. Pour into molds and place into fridge till set – 2-3 hours, or overnight
10. ENJOY!